Ozone Journal

PHOENIX POETS

PETER BALAKIAN

Ozone Journal

THE UNIVERSITY OF CHICAGO PRESS

Chicago & London

PETER BALAKIAN is the Donald M. and Constance H. Rebar Professor of the Humanities and professor of English at Colgate University. He is the author of seven books of poems, most recently of the critically acclaimed *Ziggurat*, also published by the University of Chicago Press. His memoir *Black Dog of Fate* won the PEN/Albrand Prize and was a *New York Times* Notable Book, and *The Burning Tigris: The Armenian Genocide and America's Response* was a *New York Times* best seller and a *New York Times* Notable Book.

The University of Chicago Press, Chicago 60637
The University of Chicago Press, Ltd., London
© 2015 by The University of Chicago
All rights reserved. Published 2015.
Printed in the United States of America

24 23 22 21 20 19 18 17 16 15   1 2 3 4 5

ISBN-13: 978-0-226-20703-2 (paper)
ISBN-13: 978-0-226-20717-9 (e-book)
DOI: 10.7208/chicago/9780226207179.001.0001

Library of Congress Cataloging-in-Publication Data

Balakian, Peter, 1951– author.
    Ozone journal / Peter Balakian.
        pages ; cm. — (Phoenix poets)
    Includes bibliographical references.
    ISBN 978-0-226-20703-2 (pbk. : alk. paper) —
ISBN 978-0-226-20717-9 (e-book)
    I. Title. II. Series: Phoenix poets.
    PS3552.A443O97 2015
    811'.54—dc23

                            2014016859

♾ This paper meets the requirements of ANSI/NISO Z39.48–1992
(Permanence of Paper).

for ASKOLD MELNYCZUK

CONTENTS

ACKNOWLEDGMENTS

My thanks to the editors of the magazines in which these poems, sometimes with different titles, first appeared:

Agni: "Near the Border," "Slum Drummers"
Boston Review: "Hart Crane in LA, 1927"
Carolina Quarterly: section 33 of "Ozone Journal" (as "Waking/West End Ave./1983")
Colorado Review: "Pueblo, Christmas Dance"
Consequence: "Name and Place"
Harvard Review: "Providence/Teheran '79"
Massachusetts Review: "Silk Road"
New Letters: "Home"
Ploughshares: "Pueblo 1, New Mexico"
Saveur: section 12 of "Ozone Journal" (as "Breakfast in Aleppo")
Southwest Review: "Pueblo 2, New Mexico"
Tikkun: "Joe Louis's Fist"
Virginia Quarterly Review: section 45 of "Ozone Journal" (as "Kinda Blue")

"Hart Crane in LA, 1927" also appeared on *Poetry Daily* (poems.com).
"Warhol/Mao, '72" appeared in *Poems and Their Making: A Conversation*, ed. Philip Brady (Lanham, MD: Bucknell University Press, 2015).
"Here and Now" was published in a broadside limited edition of 100 by Andrew Rippeon at the Press at Nine-Mile Swamp, Clinton, NY.
"Silk Road" was reprinted in *Poetry Daily*, April 7, 2013.

With thanks to JB, SB, DLF, DSL, ML, AM, ALM, RP, WR, BS, TS, and to Yaddo, Robert Garland, and Mary Beth Kelly for sanctuaries to write.

One

NAME AND PLACE

1.

Balak in Hebrew (devastator)—King of Moab
son of Zippor (sparrow), meaning he who was always running away
into the desert as the Israelites were fast on his back.

Angry, humiliated, full of vinegar and sap,
looking for the diviner.

2.

Balak (in Turkish, eccentric variant) meaning baby buffalo—
something forging Anatolian rivers,
Armenian fossil of the word, flushed downstream.

3.

Who drowned wading in the reeds of the Ararat plain?
There the sky is cochineal.
There the chapel windows open to raw umber and twisted goats.
There the obsidian glistens and the hawks eat out your eyes.

4.

If you thought of diaspora, you were thinking of emerald stones.
If you thought of the marshes of snails and magenta bugs,
you were wading in the reeds.

Ur: like rolling a good Merlot on the palate till it runnels up the nose.
Ah: breath of the unknown.
Tu: also, everything, self and side of mountain.

The soul sweats. The blue knifes the canyon.

In a cave, a man lived on herbs and water;
the sky's grisaille was a visitation;
the leaves were out of toot sin Jants;
the angels were alpha and omega—

5.

This road goes north—

no need to ask where you are,

sentimental pop songs are stuck in the CD shuffle

there's a valley, a river, a smoking something—

if you ask what color is the sky
can anyone say—cloudless, clotted, open?

PUEBLO I, NEW MEXICO

Between mud walls and the kiva
wind off the mesa broke his phrases,
as we walked with Billy of the Parrot Clan

and with others. The windows
melting into blowing snow and the ripped-
off split-level doors jammed on the adobes.

Out of fleeting blue, then white,
we caught bites
about the time of killing Spaniards

under the full moon,
after the medicine men were hanged
by Hernando de Ugarte y la Concha

and everyone was smashed between the mesa
and the hardened lava of the caldera,
and the Spaniards ate dogs

and roasted cowhides
till they died of black blood.

Through loud wind we heard how
a ventriloquist convinced the natives
the cross of the mission was speaking:

walk into the bullets—
and they walked into the fanatical air
where the Cruzobs ate wood

until the Virgin was cursed and let go—
and that was the beginning, and the beginning
was 1680 in the year of the friars,

the year the squash grew
out of the trellised sanctuary
where a dozen Christs were bleeding

and the after-stink of heads
rotted into the ground.

Billy said parrots were smuggled
across the Rio Grande
and then froze on the plateau

and the clan kept the name
because of the spirit-brother
of the blazing eyes.

A kid in a Broncos T-shirt
wanted a picture taken
in front of his iced-over window;

the blue-corn girls kept coming
and going as we stood there

in the snow that obscured the mission wall
and the Christmas lights

winding around the sagging turquoise
mullions of the dented windows
where the men left their marks.

The snow blanked the straw-mud walls
as we slid down the molten cliff steps

to the street where the Christmas luminaria
burned into the fissures of tumbleweed.

Nothing is written down in our culture,
Billy said. Even if imagination
is a shard of history, am I defiling it

the way the polymorphism of those birds
mimicked us with their thick tongues.
Greek soldiers carried them to war,

their wings rimed Tang pots,
the rococo ceilings of Dresden
bore their manic green.

If the parrots followed Geronimo
from Guadalupe in a dream
could we imagine that frantic air now

where Route 66 Casino rises on
red pylons that hold up the skittering dice
and the breeze of the shuffle

as we drive into the wager and stakes
of high limits, the wheels of fortune
spinning, the cash-out buttons popping,

simulacra of feathers,
silver, beads, the blur of pots
in the rearview mirror.

PUEBLO 2, NEW MEXICO

1.

The Chief said, you can't see what's beyond the mountain,
as I watched the blue shimmer-light rise
over the tables of silver and turquoise on the square.

(Plato said the soul is in balance when reason
slices appetite into a wing.)

The Chief was a woman guide, a leather-worn
native who lived without running water to live here.

2.

I was here the day after Christmas with some money,
the sky of central New York in my coat,

I was kicking up dust and bonfire ash and pine sap
in the tracks of the square where last night

the procession carried the dais under the billowing canopy,
and candles lit the Madonna's face as the hills
disappeared in the shadows of the acolytes.

(Buddha said the self is in constant movement,
suffering is necessary, social security is negligible—but useful.)

9

3.

I passed a gruesome painted
Jesus nailed to the pine slab church door.

The Chief said there was more to see beyond the mountain.
I could see a sky over formations of rock,

light hammering the kiva where the heads of slain bears were washed—
the Chief said a shaman could suck a quill from the heart,

Montezuma was killed by the stones of his own people,
an apparition of the Virgin led to a trail south of the Rio Grande.

4.

By noon shadows returned to their crevices,
a chief's blanket folded into a cliff;

I was lost in the blue veins and scree.
I rubbed my hands on fossil bones.

The horizon was turquoise, fractured blue, copper dust.

5.

I left Jesus and Montezuma mingling in the Rio Grande
and saw the sun carry its mask across the sky.

The Chief stared at me as I wrote in my notebook
until I stopped, stuffed it in my satchel, and kept walking

through the scalp houses, caves, and kiva niches—
I took in the air of stinging pine,

saw a man hang over a roof ledge
and puke to cleanse his soul.

PUEBLO, CHRISTMAS DANCE

I.

I took a wrong turn into a sun mask
on mud, into straw-glue and smashed yucca.

If you saw them rub feathers on their arms,
if the claws of bear wrapped them,

if the porcupine and badger were sewn to the skin,
if gusts of God flew into lightning-riven wood.

All morning I drove out of one life into another,
through no water and empty self;

I saw the coordinates of a masthead of a wrecked car.

My car took the curve of a curve
just past the exit to Los Alamos

where Oppenheimer said the infinite imploded finite space—
though he couldn't have imagined

the atom pressed into the cave inside the mesa
that opened into the buffalo

who could turn into a bear,
who could be the beast.

2.

She was carried between the horns of the animal.

The grass brushed the sky.
She drank from the horn

The hill swallowed the dirt,
which became a horn of water.

The horn of water was passed among many.
Many drank while a chief blew yellow powder

through an eagle-winged bone;

space dissolved into a gourd-rattle
that made me feel the heart-shake.

In the dry cold, in the catapult past Jesus
where the bones and kernels

shook in the dry skin, there was relief.
Euclidian infinity dissolved.

I could hear the end of history
in the teeth rattling inside a gourd;

for a second, blue spears
of lightning shot over three women sleeping

under the canopy of a mud house.
The sun poured on all of us.

JOE LOUIS'S FIST

1.

After the sun rose into rust between gravel and horizon,
after the scent of you oxidized the steel of my car going
into the lidocaine of the morning air as the highway slid

into northeast Detroit past Chill & Mingle,
I did a double take and took a wrong turn at Rim Repair.
(Long ago my father said I should see the fist.)

No one spoke Swahili on 12th Street, still rubble
after the blind pigs folded up.
It was a cliché of the image of itself but it was, it was

like nothing, the vacant burned-out bungalows, car parts, metal scraps,
arson jobs, abandoned homes, barbed wire playgrounds,
shacks pummeled along Six Mile Road—derelict since '67.

2.

My father said when Louis won the radio static was a wave
of sound that stayed all night like the riots blocks away in Harlem,
as the scent of lilac and gin wafted down Broadway to his window

across from the Columbia gates where the sounds of
Fletcher Henderson and Dizzy buzzed the air,
where the mock Nazi salutes were shadows over the

granite lions and snake dancing. Car horns
banged the tar and busted windshields;
even coffee shops south of 116th were looted.

3.

It came back in fragments—through the gauze
of the summer of love, through Lucy in the Sky
and other amnesias; streets of burnt-out buildings,

paratroopers bivouacked in high schools with gas and bayonets.
By 6:00 a.m. July 23 national guard were walking
in the rain of black cinder and pillars of smoke—

a black body hanging from a fence of an auto-part yard,
whisky-faced boys shooting through the fire
as torn bags of loot trailed the streets.

Prostitutes used pool cues to defend themselves.
Booze and cartridge smoke ate their skin.
One trooper said it looked like Berlin in '45.

4.

Samson, David, and Elijah in one left hook,
my father said (6/22/38), upbraided Neville Chamberlain,
liberated Austria and Sudetenland,

knocked the lights out in Berlin—
sent Polish Jews into the boulevards
for one night of phantasmal liberation.

Because Hitler banned jazz, because Black Moses led
crowds and crowds to the marvelous, inscrutable, overwhelming
balked dreams of revenge, millions seeped out of doorways, alleys, tenements—

dreaming of the diamond pots, Chrysler heaven,
the golden girls of Hollywood; Shirley Temple
rubbed some salt into his hands for luck.

Untermensch from Alabama—
sucker for the right hand—the other side of Haile Selassie;
black men howled to him from their electric chairs.

    5.

When I drove past Berry Gordy, Jr. Boulevard
and *Hitsville USA* on the studio house,
the lights were out and I could only

imagine the snake pit where Smokey Robinson
spun into vinyl, where "Heat Wave"
came as sweet blackmail in the beach air of '64,

where the Funkbrothers and Martha Reeves
took the mini opera and dumped it on its head.

By the time I hit Jefferson and Woodward
the sun was glaring on the high windows,
and then it hit me—spinning the light—

horizontal two-foot arm smashing the blue
through the empty pyramid holding it up
in the glare of skyscraper glass: molten

bronze-hand, hypotenuse of history,
displaced knuckles—

the smooth casting over the gouged-out wounds—
the naked, beloved, half-known forms.

HART CRANE IN LA, 1927

We sat in leather chairs
around cocktail tables and the candidates

came and went with badges on their jackets, proud and scared,
full of knowledge and uncertainty.

Everyone was animated as the conversation
drifted toward an idea of the idea of the text.

One colleague pointed out in an interview that it was here
right in this room under this chandelier that a poet

once came for a while in uncertainty and fear,
and that he rode into LA's great pink vacuum of

sunsets and spewed Rimbaud out on the Boulevard.
The candidates kept coming and going,

other colleagues dropped over to say hi or to chat about
the menu at the other hotel, and someone else said

that the poet loved this place and that we should stay here
where he had come to devour paté and lobster,

where Ivor Winters met him for old-fashioned cocktails
and noted later that his hands looked

like a seasoned pugilist's, his face like bad road.
Another colleague said you couldn't understand Crane's big poem

without context, the other said you couldn't understand
context without the poem. Another said, listen to the

strange sound the words make when you let the silence in.

The first colleague said the words were so clotted and glued
that it was impossible to decipher meaning, real meaning.

But someone else reminded the others that the poet
was so desperate he pawned his grandmother's watch

and then wrote to Gide, "No Paris ever yielded such as this."

Later when things got worse, when the houses
turned the color of stale mayonnaise,

he went down to the beach to read Hopkins
and claimed the drawling mockingbirds drowned out the spondees.

The first colleague said his idea of the poem was
too big for any life to carry and so the end was inevitable.

Then the waiter appeared, slightly harassed, and everyone
ordered a lobster club and a diet coke, before the next candidate arrived

as another colleague repeated, with an edge in her voice, "Inevitable?"

PROVIDENCE/TEHERAN, '79

1.

I was held together by tranquilizers and the weft of a prayer rug,
my back dislodged; all I could do was stare from the floor
at the TV screen glowing with blurred color,

my books out of reach, on the floor like Japanese fans—
the ones I had been cramming—for my prelims—
the ones—by Bill McLoughlin on American evangelicals.

I saw the Seven Seals in the neon light of the Newport Creamery,
heard trumpets of the Baptists blowing down the walls
of American cities and who was I to say—doped up

on pain killers—when the balustrade of the US embassy disappeared
in Kalashnikov smoke on the TV screen, and students broke
the gate with their signs and fists and chants in Farsi.

The camera cut to the Aya-toll-ah—the sound unrolling
like gauze in my head—was a fade-out to the voice
of the man in the next apartment reading poems to the wall.

2.

I woke in the dark to the glow of a chateau in France, where the Aya-
toll-ah—in a robe blurred in light from the camera angle—
was sending videos to Teheran. I once saw the carpets of the Pahlavi palace

in a photo my cousin took in the '60s when my uncle did business with the Shah—
the silk wavered like the voice of Begum Akhtar cracking glass,
and then champagne poured and wire slit the voices of the invisible.

By midnight I was in black space, the mullions dissolving
into nothingness, the oak floor levitating my head
into the prayer rug where flowers grew into vines.

Shadows in the mirror disappeared; nightjars fell out of the poplars
in Teheran or Providence, where I thought I saw behind the veil
of what is seen, as the angels came down on the screen.

3.

Hours later I woke to the small white pill of a sun
through a window, to students in the streets of Teheran.
I stared at my pile of books, elegant paperbacks, old library ones,

when in my thumbed-out head I heard The Beach Boys' cawing *Barbara
Ann*—then the sync shots of the TV going—*bomb-Iran* in some
echo chamber of some town in the Midwest. Whatever

the screen's daylight waveforms sent me I saw
red blindfolds wrap American faces,
iron bars of a gate twist the windows of American

exceptionalism. Morning. Morning. No dream.
The sun lit up the red brick campus; the TV bathed in light.

WARHOL/MAO, '72

When I saw his face on a wall
at a party in a parlor looking out at the Hudson,

at a fundraiser for the winter soldiers
over blocks of cheese and baguettes,

I had just come from some grainy footage
of Dien Bien Phu in a hot black room,

where the scratched print showed the hills undulating,
bodies and parachutes disappearing in jungle grass.

Between decadence and the alien
Mao was propped in yellow and rouge

with lipstick and eye shadow,
a real queen—part décor, part radical something

the American lexicon hadn't filled in yet.

From the aerial cameras
Haiphong Harbor was liquid light.

In liquid light, I saw my draft card float like a
giant litho over the highway at 79th

the letters popped—*selective service system*—
and morphed into gray rain—

anyone could have done it—
singed, blurred, laminated—

and the bartender poured me
another unidentified drink.

In the scratched cellulose nitrite, parachutes
kept drifting down on the hedges of the Laotian border.

On the wall Mao was the punctum
in rouge and yellow and smear.

Didn't every myth signify confusion?
Confucius, Charlie Chan, Chiang Kai-shek?

(An American vision of a place.)

The guy behind me in class asked,
"Where is this place?"

Hanoi was glittering flecks on the nightly news,
and the teacher answered,

"Every snake of land is someone's history."

We didn't know what we didn't know about
the backyard furnaces, the tens of millions.

Even if Mao swallowed Darwin and Adam Smith
swimming the Yangtze—here on the Upper West

in late spring, he was wallpaper,
the most recognizable face in the world.

There seemed no point in breaking through the mask—
I was glued to the colors for a while,

until the next war let us out of Asia
until the sun went down on the wall.

BASEBALL DAYS, '61

All summer the patio drifted in and out of light the color of margarine;
days were blue, not always sky blue.
At night the word Algeria circulated among the grown-ups.

A patient of my father had whooping cough, the words drifted into
summer blue. The evenings spun into stadium lights.
Kennedy's hair blew across the screen. Castro was just a sofa.

I saw James Meredith's face through a spread of leaves
on the evening news. The fridge sweat with orangeade,
the trees whooped some nights in rain—

a kid down the street kept coughing into his mitt.
Static sounds from Comiskey and Fenway came
though the vinyl, the plastic, the pillow—

So when it left Stallard's hand, when Roger Maris's arms whipped
the bat and the bullet-arc carried into the chasm of disaffections
at 344 ft. near the bullpen fence

under the green girder holding up the voices rising into the façade and over the
    river
where a Baptist choir on Lenox Ave. was sending up a variation of *Sweet Chariot*
into the traffic on the FDR that was jammed at the Triboro

where a derrick was broken and the cables of its arms picked up the star-blast of
    voices coming over the Stadium façade spilling down the black next-game
    sign into the vector
of a tilted Coke bottle on a billboard

at the edge of the river where a cloud of pigeons rose over Roosevelt Island.
It was evening by the time the cars unjammed and the green of the outfield unfroze
and the white arc had faded into skyline before fall came

full of boys throwing themselves onto the turf with inexplicable desire
for the thing promised. The going. Then gone.

Two

OZONE JOURNAL

1.

I woke to CFCs humming out of coils.

I woke to a compressor in my head
and the compressor in the wall that made cool air come out of the vents—

couldn't sleep—downloaded photos of the day,
to stare at them, as if the sky were something I could breathe in:

not good times by the sea, but—desert-blue and cracked ground,

some tumbleweed blowing into my jeans;
green signs of Arabic letters looked like beautiful tributaries,

as they faded out along a road going to the Iraqi border,

where oil refineries were firing on the horizon,
where a border is a road: ending and beginning.

2.

All day I was digging Armenian bones out of the Syrian desert

with a TV crew that kept ducking the Mukhabarat
who trailed us in jeeps and at night joined us

for arak and grilled goat under colored pennants and cracked lights
in cafés where piles of herbs glistened back at me.

I passed out from sun and arak and camel jokes

in a massive hotel, my room opened to the Euphrates
that was churning in the moonlight.

    3.

When I woke I was dreaming back to the '80s on Riverside Drive
where Ani was born on a bright spring day,

in a decade of money and velvet when the plastic voice of Sinatra
floated through fern bars where we lounged

with wine spritzers and lemon-drop martinis.
It was silver palette and more than cuisine

with its encoded sense of ending
and the smoked sable at Barney Greengrass

where we took Ani for brunch
on Sunday when the morning was lit up and open,

    4.

—dreaming back to days
(why here on the black Euphrates at 4:00 a.m.?)

after our life went up in a blue flame as the gas jet died
and—we were gone to each other—

the walls silent and the floor boards echoed;
the U-Haul came and my books got rained on—

and the flags were rippling for Saint Gennaro.
Thisbe and Pyramus disappeared as myth and symbol
and that summed it up.

5.

Those days (no dream) the squeaky cassette going—
on Jerry in Riverdale. When I arrived the sky was graphed
through phone wires and Amtrak cables.

I was sitting beneath shelves of uncut-masters—
the 78s of 1940 when Jerry cut the modern LP
and found the lost Hot Jazz of the '20s—

I was staring at hanging Armenian rugs and the river glare
on a photo of Miles Davis—almost liquid in the sepia emulsion

of 1947 when the smoke spiraled into Three Deuces on 52nd
at a table with Sterling Brown and Gillespie and Jerry—

and he put it (in his hammered speech), "John Hammond
was so hated by the musicians, Miles cut him out of the photo and pasted
Dizzy in—but that was before I got Miles interested in Cage."

6.

By noon I was leaning on the cotton white hospital wall,
gazing at the islands of purple lesions on
David's slightly swollen leg, the edema rising

in his groin, the sheets strewn and the IV
dripping blue down the snaking plastic tube.

My year of magical thinking looped down
the drain of my brain: "Take care, cousin."

I blew him a kiss,

7.

before I was back at the English department table,

feeling the post mortem of the modern:
the paradigm critique essential but the artifact
thrown out with the bathwater.

Over-fetishizing indeterminacy,
or depressed expression of late capitalism?

Get Foucault and Trilling in bed—
give peace a chance.

Gorky said, take a flat brush
and work it till there are two hairs left.

8.

Light comes diffuse out of itself over the Euphrates
from the hotel room veranda—irrigated farmland/yellow tint/
veins running through furrows/snaking green patches—

9.

and I see David's eyes flat and glassy;
his voice through Xanax

was a silk kerchief through a ring—
memory was focus, detail, the thing—

the way sun lit up brownstone—

the way a Burgundy was a whiff when the cork pops
and the air is Tiffany and evening comes

with its mix and synthesized backing tracks.

Pigeons flew into porch lanterns
and the spring synth notes of Donna Summer,

as the cold and hot pianos melted into riot bombs of
strobes and the dust of white powder:

off Columbus on 71st in the '70s.

10.

When I walked under the canopy of the Ansonia
I saw your hand in the restoration of the
turreted copper and the beaux arts angels,

the mansard roof floated in the ultra rays,

where you worked in the early '80s on the running
frieze and the cornices

while down on the sidewalk, everyone was buffed up on glistening
shops of leather, tiers of mangos, apples, honeydew.

At night Ani slept as if we were still together.
Her breathing calmed the saw that spits the air.

11.

Gray-yellow light over the river;
got a train to Riverdale and sat with Jerry over

Armenian coffee as he sorted through papers and photos
and one of Billy H. at the Three Dueces, and Jerry put it this way:

"We were there till the early light came into the club
and Miles was shaking like a paralytic"

cultivate in yourself a grand similarity
with the chaos of the surrounding ether;

unloose your mind; set your spirit free;
be still as if you had no soul.

"Miles laughed, then passed out,

that sense—of—sense of nothing—ness came
alive when we did the *Blue* sessions...."

12.

Breakfast in the van: muhammara, fig jam,
thin pita-like soft parchment;

I'm eating earth and air as I fold
it over cracked green olives—

military vehicles shedding rust—
khaki camouflage and the Assad-
faced facades looking back at us.

     13.

I watched David's Buddhist
gaze as he imagined how—

how the body turned on itself and the virus
spiked its protein into T cells

(he was drawing on napkins: CD4/CD8)

"that summer we complained of coughs,
numb skin in spots in early evening

when the Lux filled up and the homeless came to Gray's Papaya—"

he kept talking through the beep of the IV;
at noon the nurses wheeled in some trays.

     14.

On the days when the rings on our fingers hurt,
I drifted into the white noise of the crowd
on the turned-up TV; no need for Stoli—

the field cam gaze brought me the dazzling green
white lines/foul pole/second-base glistening,
the green transfixing like money.

The heroes haunting us after the game—
the idea of glory rubbing off

on our shirts like angel dust;
anyone lost in the crowd

is born again in the after-image
of buoyancy and beer—

the ego dissolving into victory over death
for a day, or a moment of certainty,

as Camus once put it:

"if only once it could be said: *this is clear*—
then all would be saved."

15.

Speeding by al-Raqqah, appearing, disappearing—
the idea of Babylon, Assyria, Sumer:
an abstraction of sun on water—

toward Margadeh—smell of sand storm rising—
caves appearing, disappearing into stone huts of light.

16.

The present kept sliding into David's past,
unraveling through drip-drugs and sedatives.

I heard a version of the Upper West at a moment
when history was an image caught in a pincer:

morning was blood orange on Columbus Ave.
evening was a rum punch and then

a riot of Quiana collars/blow and poppers
arms and legs of Jell-O in the stairwells
where Calvin Klein disappeared like a holy ghost,

and out there in the American day—Terrence Malick's light
spread on the libidinal wheat and rutted prairie—

that was the '70s: post-Nixon
euphoria, pre-Khomeini inflation of the soul
over the Williamsburg Bridge at midday

the full-throated wobbly sax
of Sonny Rollins when everyone was
a bachelor with a PhD in anthro or comp lit,

17.

and then I was hunched under the celeb photos on the wall
over an absurd pile of pastrami at the Carnegie, and a snippet
fell out of my notebook: "The measurements onboard the *Nathaniel B. Palmer*

showed that a one-hour exposure to light that is similar
to the sun under the ozone hole is enough to completely stop all
photosynthetic activity of the plankton"

no plankton, no world: who can take in the dread—

already late to pick up Ani at dance class—

     18.

Jerry believed what the Greeks believed: sound had color

and what Miles said: "the softer you play, the stronger it gets"

when I got home my daughter's voice was skidding
along the fluctuating magnetic signal of the answering machine—

loneliness droned me to the beep, lulled me to sleep

     19.

before I woke to hammered silver air over the river—

fish-eye sun—irascible, hardtack, scarred, and varnished,

ozone: major factor in making life on earth possible;
O_3—allotropic, oxidizing, disinfectant, poisonous;
pale blue gas, sharp, irritating—ignited by UV rays.

20.

Obsessive angles of light off stone,
5:00 a.m., camera crew: M. and B. brilliant
making the narrative hang in the/blind

/white/punctum

boom mike dangles/a huge mouth—
in sun—

21.

the UV trance taking me back to
T cells floating in the elevator at Saks,
spikes of protein/genome invasion—

between Chernobyl and Bhopal
AIDS became gossip, evasion, denial.

22.

We were walking our Friday ritual
over the GW, the lights of Midtown burning—

we were buzzed on nothing,
the nothing of the night sky half-smogged
with wavering lights on the cables,

buzzed on water from a wooden bowl,
a liquor never brewed;

I could keep saying it, even if the lines
were from the greats of the American sublime,
because our wine never grew in the belly of the grape.

23.

When the driver stopped for arak at a gas station the color of
pomegranates/smeared plums/Syrian lavender/
I was texting Ani back in Boston—the send-icon spinning nowhere.

24.

On Sundays I came to the hospital with café au lait and choreg—

David was all memory as if a little Madeleine were floating in tea:

outside of a jazz club in Beyoğlu, Turkey—he told me:

Alan (the love of my life) was ranting (why there, why then?)

about the wall that came down
at Stonewall, before we all/

and then/and how/

the Humpty Dumpy faggot cops, handcuffed women,
Van Ronk and company too.

Fairies weren't supposed to fight back;

someone doused the bar with lighter fluid—
the street was Jackson Pollock smashed,
pay phones toilets jukebox cigarette machines—

we hung our peacock-embellished texts
on the graffiti-ripped plaster of Christopher Street

spectral emanations rose off the curb.

And here we were standing under the Turkish street light,
charred lamb in the air;
we chugged our scotch and

and back we went inside the club with
a couple of Kurdish guys

and later near dawn set out to find
the wall on the Bosphorus

where our family house once was.

25.

When the slamming light came over the buttes and oil towers
the Euphrates went strange pewter—

sound of planes droned out
over the Iraqi border—

where the green zones blanked into car bombs,
blast-wall T-hit barbed-wire;

the Tigris was fire and Babylonian bricks;
through the chained acres of ruined silt
sheep were driven into the Kurdish north.

26.

We strollered over the river,
as the ultraviolet rays split off chlorine atoms,

Ani wrapped in infant pink and white;

at 161st we found the bleachers
where the lights blinded the moths.

Dominican boys ran from scalpers/MLB
cowhide on the hand and heart—

Later, walking back over the Macomber Bridge—
chlorine monoxide left us lighter.

27.

"Down at Café Bohemia,"

Jerry was talking slow now/the light going fast
into the violet-gray river air (I'd been there for hours),

"we started recording"—

(the primitive cassette squeaking and sliding)

"in late '55—after the third session,
Miles said, 'anything goes, but only when nothing is taken as the basis'—

sounded like baked-over Cage to me:

a source for the cool, for miles ahead,
for his fastidious dragged air."

            28.

Women along the roadside in black—
wrapped in black—I thumbed it on my iPhone.

Past the massive walls of the Aleppo Citadel,
wrapped in black.

I dozed in the throaty dust of Arabic and Armenian
coming off cell phones in the front seat.

            29.

Memory was someone's history: private, political, social—
so I remember the ginkgo twisted out of the sidewalk by our door,

second nature of light—light of spectrum and love—
light of Grünewald halo

blew through us as we walked across Sheep Meadow

just outside the violet end of infrared at sunset.

Ani kept demanding soft ice cream.
I carried her on my shoulders till dark.

30.

News pouring off telex blur of screen color on iPhone,

old *Chaldean bricks washed into the Tigris,*
the cylinder seals—pieces of Ur gone—

still trying to text Ani in Boston.

31.

I walked in with two coffees in Styrofoam—still black over
the Hudson, a stalled out Amtrak car under the rail lamp—

Jerry hoarse and whispering:

"I'm here—here—because of 92 bales of rugs that sailed out of Tabriz.

And by the time we moved to 3rd Ave. the sound was coming to me. Coming
    through warps
and wefts. A man stood on a tenement roof in the black air;

I heard the impulse shoot through water towers and fire escapes;
Fats Waller was clear from WLW Cincinnati after midnight

when my parents spoke another language in another room;
the Persian tiles glistened; the floor was flower hieroglyphs—"

32.

green zone flitting like digital dots in the rearview mirror,

the camera crew got: severe/soft/breaking/light/5:00 a.m.;

our vans drifted past some ruins and caves—through it.

33.

Back then—we woke to exhaust fumes.
You came in with espresso and a bowl of berries.

By noon I could see the yellow haze on the Jersey side.
Bach's cantata in B-flat minor in the cassette,
we lounged under the greenhouse-sky, the UVBs hacking
at the acids and oxides and then I could hear the difference

between an oboe and a bassoon
at the river's edge under cover—
trees breathed in our respiration;

there was that something on the other side of the river,
something both of us were itching toward—

radical bonds were broken, history became science.
We were never the same.

34.

To articulate the past historically (as Walter B. put it), after midnight on

the D from Flushing, crammed between two kids—

does not mean to recognize it the way it really was.

"I can feel it in the air tonight, O Lord," the boom box at the stop at 59th—

it means to seize hold of a memory as it flashes up at the moment of danger—

35.

Back then we walked through over-burnished hanging wares
into CNN and Nintendo.

Ani and her friends huddled over icons on

a Mac and the real became
MS-DOS chipped into the ministry

of arbitrage in the middle of Reaganism
in some elusive embrace in our new stuffed interiors.

36.

"On a freezing night in January (I was 17) helping Benny Goodman
who was playing for the Spanish Loyalists at Columbus Circle,

I got Lionel Hampton's xylophone and Gene Kruppa's drums into a taxi,

cut my hand on the xylophone; the blood froze on the keys all the way up 6th Ave.
Inside a makeshift room I was the Jew, the Armenian, the horn-rimmed kid from

prep school they thought was him, and they handed me a glass; they called for
    him who
hadn't arrived, and so I raised a glass and shouted 'Muerte a Franco!'

The room peeled with joy, the lights smoked up, the grappa burned me down,

Peggy Lee appeared out of the smoke; down the edge of a dark wall bodies
drifted through space, the winds hustled four to the bar—we were the red hordes

turning Catalonia into the American thing, into the mistral where the guns
    drowned
in the erratic tempo of waves, into the arms and legs that wrapped me up all night—"

37.

While our friends in Tribeca were buzzed
on other stuff we were sucked up in our belief—
as the bird-dazzled clouds hit the ridge
and the ripe river air dissolved the bridge—

our belief—in Dylan Thomas's thunderous cadences
like backed-up water let loose over a barricade

as we went down by the riverbank
and were mad for the atmosphere,

the collision, the sweetest of entries,

the long pulsations before the sun broke
in our heads like Grünewald's yellow on the face of Jesus—

47

under the Palisades at the Boat Basin
looking up at the Bridge, at the Deco girders,

dreaming of the Algonquin and Edmund Wilson
in 1930 when the river was bridgeless at the Jersey

spot. Down there—we were the bottom
of the bowl, the sedimentary rock rolled

and the words were hulls of boats lapped by water.

    38.

I walked around between classes imagining T-4 counts,

two white-banded blue capsules every 4 hrs.

later in the day, I rolled up my sleeve

and the nurse asked,
are you gay?
No.
Have you ever shared a needle with anyone?
No.
Have you had any intimate contact with anyone
who has AIDS or has been exposed to HIV?
No.
Sir, you need a psychiatrist, not a blood test.

39.

Syphilis is a punishment God has reserved for our Late Ages (Cotton Mather)

or—history is, as Defoe put it: "the fate of
things gives a new face to things."

I plugged that into the '80s

after Jerry Falwell said, *AIDS is God's judgment for a society that does not live
    by His Rules*—

40.

the new idea—The Blue—that Jerry claimed
came out of Cage with its modality of stretching time

to take the Greek idea of fusion of color and sound

which is what I felt as I walked south after
the department meeting—

into the hour when time becomes light:
the chalice of the Chrysler Building goes platinum,

the river starts dusting down
for bridge lights and traffic;

accretion, enumeration, excess
giving way to wrecked solitude

and an idea of late day
this day and after and after

after teaching, after the chalkboard
staring back at me

and light warping
through the glass of Grand Central:

everything goes cobalt of Bohemia,
Persian lapis, the Virgin's cloak—

color of longing over mountains;

that's how he drained his trumpet.

    41.

aerosols, river haze, CS gas, we moved
with whatever floats—dispersions of self and industrial manna,
the shirtless exiles walking up 158th

along the river where your jewelry was stolen in an apartment
with jerry-rigged fire escapes, an inside job done by
mild-mannered tenants who disappeared into soot fumes

and the nanoparticles of spray-can mist;
by the time we realized what happened
they were in another state.

    42.

At the caves.
M. is obsessed with light flickering down—
affect of the punctum:

while remaining a detail, the space fills up the whole picture.

M. *Were thousands of Armenians stuffed in here?*
B. *Fisk called them primitive gas chambers.*

M. drops the boom mic into darkness; sand floats through light-chipped space.

If you try to imagine death here, the detail is not the whole—the whole disappears.
The cave is a black gullet swallowing itself—

43.

David was living under scabs,
riveted by his past, and going north

on the A Train I was reading
Defoe's *Journal of the Plague Year*:

following the London streets as they break apart into back alleys
and mews, intersecting circles, a broken lane sliced by
a carriage wheel—and there I found one intersection

between word and thing at Bishopsgate Cemetery
as it hooks into clumps of green before it's wiped out

by piles of rotting bodies and a compost of
souls who begat themselves to the other (London, 1720).

When I get out in the bright light of the sidewalk
words are dissolving into objects and air
and the DNA that's zinged by ultraviolet, infra-CO_2;

scribbled in my Penguin edition:
"dangerous times/see clearly."

      44.

Walking past the San Remo
that day, I was beginning to see history

as images filtered through cracked glass—
and then I heard sirens and watched a crowd

swell into the park.

Before the infrared spread over the mansard
of the Ansonia

I was back at the sink
my face slicing into surfaces
as the knife slits a kiwi

and the pubic fuzz
rubbed off in my palms

when it appeared on the screen:
Lennon's body on the sidewalk by the Dakota gate.

You called me from work,
your voice almost inaudible;

45.

that's how the sound floated
in a noisy bistro—

the muted frequency froze me—
Jimmy Cobb's brushes were fine sand

blowing over glass—
blowing off into empty—

slow and strange, Count Basie said about *Kinda Blue*—
(not like the frantic bebop on-the-road).

It should be passé now
but the austere mute, wavering

alienated half valves,
needled the nerves between two boroughs.

The glasses clink with various mediocre
wines; plates of poached salmon blur.

46.

By '83 T-cell syndrome was graffiti on the brain;

it wasn't a second Nineveh but the zodiac read: Peking leprosy,
simian plague/Zaire/bubos/rat.

47.

Carrying dirt, rocks, bone fragments in my hands back to the van;

sun = total; Bedouin on the roadside herding sheep, women wrapped in ab-ex
colors;

I'll tell you I was here but you won't believe me; the camera crew wasn't
imitating Orpheus.

48.

On Sunday—I stared at the closed curtain as the sharagans drifted into myrrh

under the gold-leaf Armenian dome on 34th and 2nd—
when you and Ani slept late—

havedanius havedaneetz to the memory of Anatolian church windows that had
no glass
where the hawks glide out of the blue into silver lamps

(the priest repeated the graffiti on the subway wall:
Jesus hates corporate greed).

The frankincense trailed me out to the street—

the dim sum already out,
the bad coffee drifting across 34th.

I slipped into a cab to the hospital

was thinking:

49.

via negativa—

feast on Grünewald's Christ,
ignominious, bitter, the lacerated skin,

dislocated joints on the rack,
gashes on the underside of the feet—

where the nails tore away the physics of the known—

take it beyond compassion and pity
to the awful real—

50.

Oil-rig flames in distance on Iraqi border—
gray-violet light dissolves the desert and the order;

Il y a longtemps que j'taime—

now the sky: black—and teal;
then the moon: vacant, white, unreal—

51.

That day as I was leaving—
David tossed me his amulet—

"Use it for me"—

I stared at *abra* and *cadabra*,
the lingering Aramaic

set into tesserae so the
word-sound could be action

and the sound-word could be hope.

I walked out of the hospital—
the air scrolled into itself,
the sky kissed my pores—

Who are you? the white bird asked,

Less—

52.

Carved head of Abraxas,
grazed it with my thumb:

head of a cock, body of a man,
serpent legs, wielding a club and shield.

The etched-away gold leaf
smooth and slightly ridged,

bought in a shop by Alan
(who died two years later) near the Park Hotel

where our great uncle from Buenos Aires introduced tango
to the Turks in '32, where Kemal

sat over gin and wine week after
week transfixed by the open
and closed embrace of the Argentine

2/4—4/4 as the seams of stockings
glazed the open floor and the neon
bar was almost lost in smoke.

I rubbed that Nilotic coin
into my thumb until the
two were one.

I wore it around my neck
in smog and sun.

53.

I still have the note Jerry left me on graph paper—
"In utter emptiness, anything can take place"—Cage.

54.

Half-light of morning
floating over the Euphrates;

long breath in: warm black:
slow breath out—cool blue.

If you feel the emptiness, you can see anything:
be in it: as matter, as matter of fact.

Three

HERE AND NOW

The day comes in strips of yellow glass over trees.

When I tell you the day is a poem
I'm only talking to you and only the sky is listening.

The sky is listening; the sky is as hopeful
as I am walking into the pomegranate seeds
of the wind that whips up the seawall.

If you want the poem to take on everything,
walk into a hackberry tree,
then walk out beyond the seawall.

I'm not far from a room where Van Gogh
was a patient—his head on a pillow hearing
the mistral careen off the seawall,

hearing the fauvist leaves pelt
the sarcophagi. Here and now

the air of the tepidarium kissed my jaw
and pigeons ghosting in the blue loved me

for a second, before the wind
broke branches and guttered into the river.

What questions can I ask you?
How will the sky answer the wind?

The dawn isn't heartbreaking.
The world isn't full of love.

SLUM DRUMMERS, NAIROBI

1.

What were we watching on the tube under mildewed ceilings in Eastlands?
A Kenyan guy shaking a rattle made from a can
while another guy in the band was talking to the queen

about making sound out of anything? The queen smiled.
The Jubilee receiving line filed through.

2.

We shimmied past tin shacks selling wigs and bananas, coke and goat lungs;

the tine of a kalimba kissed my face. My face kissed the blue plastic of
a soda bottle sliding down a hill of glass.

I paid the gang leaders for protection
and we walked into the hills of airplane garbage,

black and blue plastic bags glowing in the sun spray over the heads
of the marabou stalking the mounds with their knife-blade beaks.

3.

Stevie Wonder and Elton John moved through the Jubilee line.
Prince Charles thanked God for the weather as the camera cut

63

to fireworks spewing over Hyde Park and then to an image of Nairobi
and the Slum Drummers picking metal out of the collages of garbage.

4.

My jeans were charred from the tin-can fires,
and the grilling pig guts when some men looked up from scraps of wire—

and you went back and forth with them in Swahili before they offered us
some sizzling fat, before we thanked them with our coy smiles and moved on
    with Michael who took us

down a maze of alleyways where tin shacks were floating
on polymers and nitrogen and a dozen pigs from nowhere snouted the garbage.

5.

You were saying "Dad"—when a marabou-hacked bag shot some shit
on our shoes—"Dad, kinship roles are always changing"—

when a woman asked us for a few shillings and salt
for her soup. Salt? Did I hear her right? Or was it Swahili
for something else? And through the sooty wind of charcoal fires

and creaking rusty tin you were saying, "Hannah Arendt called Swahili
a degraded language of former slave holders."

In the soot of my head—I was listening—
and Michael was asking for more shillings for the gang guys

who were "a little fucked up," he said, "but needed help"—
and when I turned around the heads of chickens

were twitching, the feathers fluttering down on oozing sludge;
"Arendt called it *a nineteenth century kind of no language,*"

you were saying, "*spoken*"—as we were jolted
by a marabou eating a shoe—"*spoken—by the Arab ivory and slave caravans.*"

6.

Out of bottles, cans, pipes, mangled wire—the Slum Drummers
twisted and hacked, joined and seamed their heaven

into the black plastic ghost of a mashed pot.
Pure tones blew from the vibrato holes

like wind through Makadara
where the breath of God flew through sewage pipes.

I heard in a tubophone the resurrection
of ten men rising out of coal and pig snouts

into the blue Kenyan sky where a marabou

swallowed a purse—and a woman's conga
was parting at the seams above boiling soup cans.

7.

Down a slope of stinking plastic you kept on about Arendt—
"a hybrid mixture of Bantu with enormous Arab borrowings"

I could say *poa poa   sawa sawa   karibu.*

We could make a kalimba out of a smashed pot
and pour beans into a can and shake it for the queen.

Yesterday in the soundless savannah the wildebeests and zebras
seemed to float through the green-gold grass toward Tanzania.

We could hear a lion breathe; we could hear wind through tusks.

8.

On TV the guys were grinning into metal go-go drums;
hammering twisted sewage pipes and cut wire like sailors from Mombasa—
harder nailed than da Gama's voyage down the Arab trade coast—

9.

So, where are we—in a slum of no language?
Walking through steam shovels of light, breaking over
mounds of metal as if the sky were just blue plastic?

Isn't English just a compost heap of devouring grammar,
joined, hacked, bruised words, rotting on themselves?

I keep following you, daughter of scrutiny, into plastic fields of carrion

between sight and site, vision not visionary, pig guts on the grill,

trying to keep balance
between streams of sewage and the sky,

as you keep hacking, Sophia, at the de-centered,
the burning text, anthropology's shakedown.

A marabou just knifed the arm of a woman picking
bottles out of plastic bags.

A rooster crows from under a pile
of galvanized tin as if it were morning on a farm.

LEAVING ALEPPO

How did the sound of bells come over the cliffs
when the silks on the racks strangled the air—
before they turned to clouds of flowers?

That's how the day came with its pomegranate seeds
and street screams; the priest who walked us last night
through the Armenian quarter was missing by noon.

The sky over the courtyard of Forty Martyrs Church
was frozen blue, ringing with AK-47s
and bells that my grandmother heard in another day.

We left our bags in the bedroom and wound
up in the boom-box café where workers in camouflage
slumped over coffee and sweet pistachios.

We rolled some parchment-thin pita
in our pockets, grabbed the cracked olives.

You ran into an empty building; I stayed
until the jeeps and soldiers left and some
of my Armenian friends came out with jars of water.

A tank was rusted out—some cameras were still hanging
from fences. Some fences rolled along the horizon.

NEAR THE BORDER

(Gyumri, Armenia 12/18/10)

I.

Over brandy at breakfast we were talking about the Hellenic temple
at the edge of the canyon, and the sun gods

who were worshipped there before the time of borders and decrees.
And then the priest came and we were off in a white van

that slid into the sky that was washed into gullies
slate-gray-tarnished-silver, then smooth as tarmac just poured, the way

12/7/88 poured on the screen with numbers when I was teaching in London
and walking King's Road every day into early dark.

It wasn't until we got to Gyumri and you put it casually over pizza: you
were in shop class shaving a hammer in a drill press and the floor began to slide.

2.

The neon lights glared over our faces as the amped-up
Russian waitress with green hair spilled coke on the table.

I remember 12/7/88 the Albert Bridge lit up and the Thames smooth black—
    as I watched walls come down on the screen;

a man carried a child through a gouged-out apartment,
three women passed with sacks into the stone dust and became damask.

69

———

The neon lights in the pizza place on the square flashed on the window
as you pointed out the rebuilt school and hotel and the polished tufa stone

of fault-line resistance. Outside we picked up the teenage boy,
who settled into the front seat with the priest; a medley of punk

was a soft buzz off the rattling speakers, and the priest began talking to the boy
    in medias res
about how the body and soul must find a balance with each other,

if we're to make our own destiny, God couldn't do it all for you.

———

It came back to you in spurts—
how the floor dished you into the hall, the hammer shaving your hand as

a wall seemed to throw you into the street
where mattresses and chairs were sandwiched in crushed cars.

3.

I was chewing a pizza crust as we walked through abandoned fields of Stalin
    barracks.
Under the Soviet eagles and busted windows along the tracks where Near East
    Relief

trains once arrived with powdered milk and clothes for the orphans in the '20s—
we kicked some rusted cans. Armenian soldiers went back and forth at the

checkpoints of a new history; three women with bags disappeared
into the fog along a chain-link fence.

4.

Memory is like the hammer you used to make coffins
all week with your uncle. When you found your cousins under

rubble they were speaking clearly through the dark—but that was early in the day.
On the BBC some faces moved along the street, the sun lit up punched-out
    windows

of Brezhnev-buildings, in the morning I went to Heathrow to help load planes
    with clothes and food;
in evening at a pub off Cheyne Walk, the TV flashed casualty numbers on the
    telex

news band and the voice of Roy Orbison, who was dead at 52, stayed in my head
    all day.

5.

I was blind-sided by the sign—30 kilometers *ANI*
where the border slid into Turkey and the open plain was bleached—

a few boulders, some cattle, and beyond the tenth-century city of Ani
was a mislabeled ruin cordoned off by barbed wire, a river, and some Turkish
    guards.

6.

Between Armenia and Turkey, on the shrinking blue horizon—I saw,

but what does it mean to say "I saw"? Just the mind leveraging
a way out of confinement of a cigarette-smoke-filling van?

I saw pillars dissolving under the dome of a basilica,
some women disappearing into the abyss of Saint Gregory

as we moved through gullies and blanched grass,

7.

and the van swerved to miss some cows on the road, grazed a fence.
The priest was going on about the soul made flesh—I almost

interrupted him to ask, "the soul, not the word?" The boy nodded as he kept beat
to the Clash that was wavering from the dashboard: London was a buzz-saw drone,

hard sexual fetish, world warning; the horizon was white-air gaps now,
a flaking Virgin on a conical roof floated in the sky, and then the winds changed—

8.

The priest said to the boy that Ani was the Florence of Armenia—"lost"—he said
    it again, "lost"—and the
boy asked, really rifled back, as he lit another cigarette, why Armenia

didn't have a covenant with God like the Jews did. The priest was upset—visibly,
    in the face, like cold
wind hit through the window—and he answered in Armenian—

(my voice stalled and I didn't ask, "What are you saying?")

9.

The Sex Pistols chanted off-key like urban monks in leather,

the van jolting over ruts,

the gray light giving way to fine snow coming west from Kars.

10.

"Byron thought the Garden of Eden circled Ani and on south"—I interrupted
    the priest—
"Yes, yes, Byron learned our language"—he shot back.

"Just a romantic orientalist," I croaked—

"What?"—the priest turned and stared at me over the headrest.

"You think anything's left there? After 1915?" The CD player skipped on a
    scratch as

11.

the boy popped a can of Diet Sprite, and said something back to the priest in
    Armenian,

before we stalled in a gully and the van doors slid open and the cold rushed

us as we spilled outside with flashlights; the opaque white light blew back at me,

12.

the priest pulled his black hood up, which flashed against the white outcroppings
    on the plain that could've been sheep carcasses or something else—

The banging gonzo drums of time kept playing off the dashboard—
snow came like crazed moths.

FINCHES

In the morning there were yellow heads
and purple throats at the window;

by noon the sun had obliterated
Charlotte Delbo's frozen mud.

The stamens opened to our faces;
the rug licked us with apricots—unnamed

berries flew into cypress trees
and the pearly stalks grazed my thighs,

before the plucked strings of bird-tongues
peeled down our ears.

The circuits sizzled the big purple lips of clematis.
St. Elmo's light zinged my funny bone.

Days later when I'm alone in my bed,
holes in the sky open, then close.

SILK ROAD

for Agha Shahid Ali (1949–2002)

I drove in snow to Clinton.
My car slid into a field of buried stubble
and cows disappeared in drifts

the color of your Dacca gauzes, which were next
to nothing; for you they were all summer,
where the sun came like hammered gold on a broken dome.

You wrapped a shredded paisley—vermillion,
madder, cochineal—in a rag-worn prayer rug
I left in your car—for your trip to summer over there.

The white-out turned the bridge into a road
north to where Armenia was just a giant step
and bodies were ploughed crystal.

———

We drove from Bollywood to Deansboro
for scotch, and then the road turned
and you were driving through an undivided Punjab

where the wheat flared all summer
and you floored your Peugeot
outside of Amritsar, that city of red silk

and gold from which the road north took you
to almost nothing—where silk worms disappeared
in rotting leaves and the voice of Begum Akhtar

was stinging air as you crossed the border
into your mother's monsoon, which in Urdu
meant divergence and convergence of surface—

heating air, and there and there and there
where the road sped up the way our extravagant passions
burn the esoteric leaves that fry our wires

till the car door opens and we're sucked out
into the unknown clouds over Kolkata
where the waterlogged slums are flooded

in the brain. That was your storm
of bangles, broken ghazal lines on prison walls,
vanishing elephants that were ploughed crystal.

———

Shahid: *beloved* in Persian, *witness* in Arabic, you drove back
in the early upstate spring on the road to Hamilton
where the cows stared blankly at your car;

the mud fields were plain and cold,
potholes smashed the tires,
the road was next to nothing,

and you asked me—staring through the window
at the trees and back roads: how can gray
drizzly light, just be gray drizzly light.

HOME

Driving Route 20 to Syracuse past pastures of cows and falling silos

you feel the desert stillness near the refineries at the Syrian border.

Walking in fog on Mecox Bay, the long lines of squawking birds on shore,

you're walking along Flinders Street Station, the flaring yellow stone and walls
of windows where your uncle landed after he fled a Turkish prison.

You walked all day along the Yarra, crossing the sculptural bridges with their
twisting steel,

the hollow sound of the didgeridoo like the flutes of Anatolia.

One road is paved with coins, another with razor blades and ripped condoms.

Walking the boardwalk in January past Atlantic City Hall, the rusted Deco
ticket sign, the waves black into white,
you smell the grilled ćevapi in the Baščaršija of Sarajevo,

and that street took you to the Jewish cemetery where the weeds grew over
the slabs and a mausoleum stood intact.
There was a trail of carnelian you followed in the Muslim quarter of Jerusalem

and picking up those stones now, you're walking in the salt marsh on the
potato fields,
the day undercut by the flatness of the sky, the wide view of the Atlantic, the
cold spray.

Your uncle stashed silk and linen, lace and silver in a suitcase on a ship that
     docked not far from here; the ship moved in and out of port for years, and
     your uncle kept coming

and going, from Melbourne to London to Kolkata and back, never returning to
     the Armenian village near the Black Sea.

The topaz ring you passed on in a silver shop in Aleppo appeared on Lexington
     off 65th;
the shop owner, a young guy from Ivory Coast, shrugged when you told him you
     had seen it

before; the shuffled dust of that street fills your throat and you remember how a
     slew of
coins poured out of your pocket like a slinky near the ruined castle now a disco in

Thessaloniki where a young girl was stabbed under the strobe lights—lights that
     lit the

sky that was the iridescent eye of a peacock in Larnaca at noon, when you walked
     into the

church where Lazarus had come home to die and you forgot that Lazarus died

because the story was in one of your uncle's books that were wrapped in
     newspaper in a suitcase and
stashed under the seat of an old Ford, and when he got to the border

he left the car and walked the rest of the way, and when you pass the apartment

on 116th and Broadway—where your father grew up (though it's a dorm now)—
that suitcase is buried in a closet under clothes, and when you walk past the
   security guard

at the big glass entrance door, you're walking through wet grass, clouds
   clumped on a hillside, a subway station sliding into water.

NOTES

"Pueblo 1, New Mexico": for Sarah Wider.

"Joe Louis's Fist": for Mel Watkins.

"Hart Crane in LA, 1927": for John Naughton.

"Providence/Teheran, '79": for Mary Paula Hunter and Rich Meckel.

"Warhol/Mao, '72": for John Knecht.

"Baseball Days, '61": for Mike Holtzman.

"Ozone Journal," sections 5, 27, 31, and 36: for George Avakian.
"Ozone Journal," sections 40 and 45: for Michael Coyle and Kara Rusch.

"Slum Drummers, Nairobi": for Sophia and Michael.

"Leaving Aleppo": for Tom Sleigh.

"Near the Border": for Hayk Demoyan.

———

Joe Louis's Fist: a twenty-four-foot long arm weighing 8,000 pounds and
   rising up twenty-four feet in downtown Detroit.

"Ozone Journal": In the spring of 2009 I went with a TV crew from CBS/
   "60 Minutes" to do a segment on the Armenian genocide and in par-
   ticular to uncover the remains of Armenian skeletons in the northern
   Syrian desert of Der Zor where more than 400,000 Armenians died
   in the 1915–16 period of Turkish mass killing. One thread of this poem
   takes off on that journey—I emphasize that it takes off on the experience
   (as a poem is not a memoir)—transforming various moments into flecks
   and fragments, as the journey in Syria becomes the point of perspective

for the persona's "dreaming back" in the rest of the poem. Many thanks to that incomparable crew and to three artists, each extraordinary in his own way: Bob Simon, Michael Gavshon, and Jeff Fager.

"Slum Drummers, Nairobi": Slum Drummers of Kenya is a community-based group of young drummers who make their musical instruments from scrapped materials. In 2012 they performed for the queen of England during her birthday Diamond Jubilee concert in London.

The following sources have been helpful, and several quoted passages are self-evident: Daniel Defoe's *A Journal of the Plague Year*; Walter Benjamin's "Theses on the Philosophy of History" from *Illuminations*; John Cage's "For a Speaker" from *Silence*; Annika Nilsson's *Ultraviolet Reflections*; Susan Sontag's *AIDS and Its Metaphors*. For section 48: *havedanius havedaneetz*, Armenian, the closing of the Lord's Prayer, "unto eternity of eternities."